THE CITY LIBRARY
SPRINGFIELD, (MA) CITY LIBRARY

EMILY'S
PLACE FOR
CHILDREN

Building Character

Being Fair

by Penelope S. Nelson

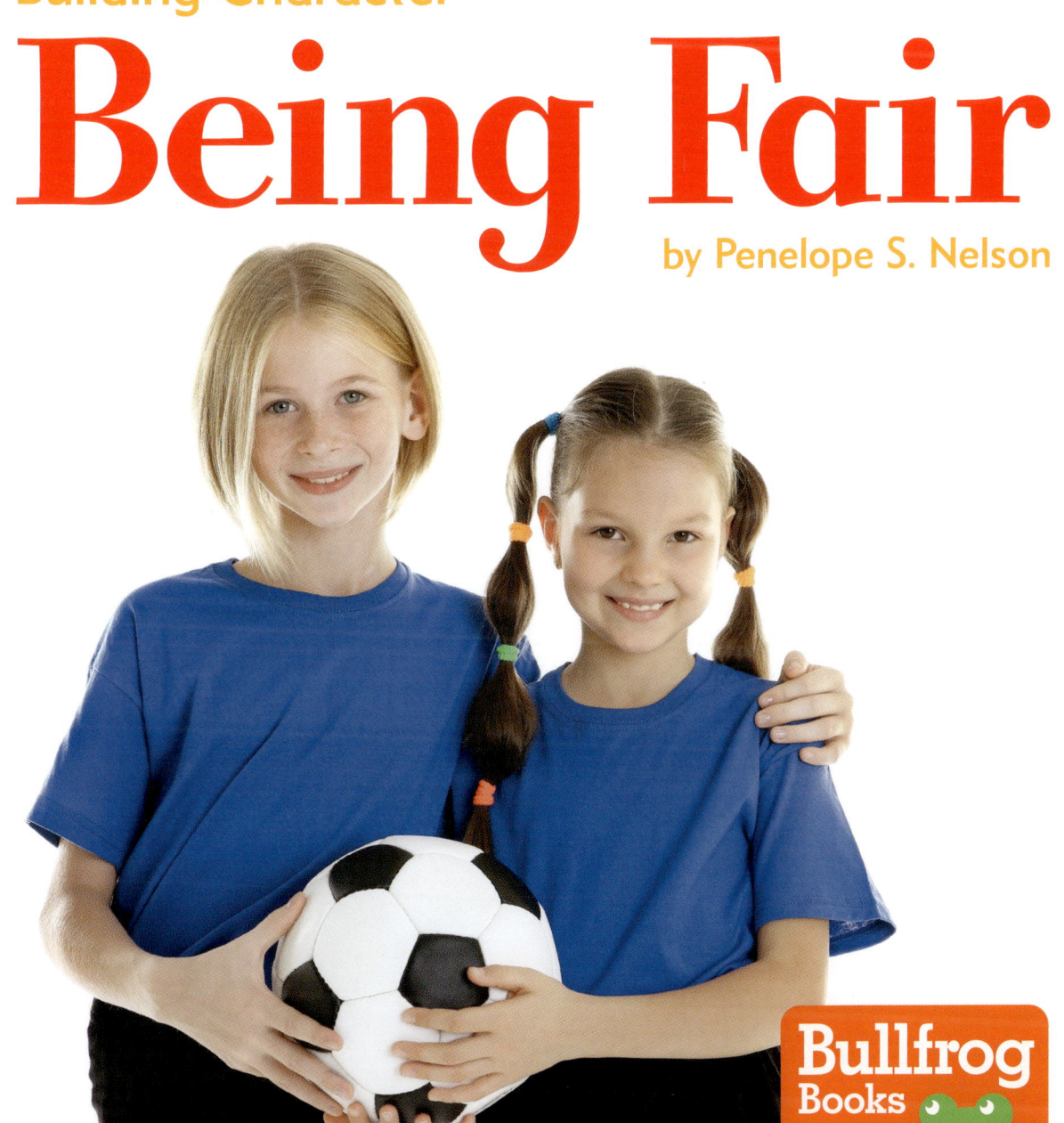

Bullfrog Books

Ideas for Parents and Teachers

Bullfrog Books let children practice reading informational text at the earliest reading levels. Repetition, familiar words, and photo labels support early readers.

Before Reading
- Discuss the cover photo. What does it tell them?
- Look at the picture glossary together. Read and discuss the words.

Read the Book
- "Walk" through the book and look at the photos. Let the child ask questions. Point out the photo labels.
- Read the book to the child, or have him or her read independently.

After Reading
- Prompt the child to think more. Ask: Can you think of a time when something was unfair? How could it have been made fair?

Bullfrog Books are published by Jump!
5357 Penn Avenue South
Minneapolis, MN 55419
www.jumplibrary.com

Copyright © 2020 Jump! International copyright reserved in all countries. No part of this book may be reproduced in any form without written permission from the publisher.

Library of Congress Cataloging-in-Publication Data

Names: Nelson, Penelope, 1994– author.
Title: Being fair / by Penelope S. Nelson.
Description: Minneapolis, MN: Jump!, Inc., [2020]
Series: Building character | Audience: Ages 5–8
Audience: Grades K to Grade 3
Includes bibliographical references and index.
Identifiers: LCCN 2018050109 (print)
LCCN 2018053625 (ebook)
ISBN 9781641287104 (ebook)
ISBN 9781641287081 (hardcover: alk. paper)
ISBN 9781641287098 (pbk.)
Subjects: LCSH: Fairness—Juvenile literature.
Classification: LCC BJ1533.F2 (ebook)
LCC BJ1533.F2 N43 2020 (print) | DDC 179/.9—dc23
LC record available at https://lccn.loc.gov/2018050109

Editor: Jenna Trnka
Designer: Michelle Sonnek

Photo Credits: Veja/Shutterstock, cover; Africa Studio/Shutterstock, 1; LightField Studios/Shutterstock, 3 (left); Viktoriia Hnatiuk/Shutterstock, 3 (right); Ko Backpacko/Shutterstock, 4; gchutka/iStock, 5, 23bl; wavebreakmedia/Shutterstock, 6–7, 20–21, 23tr; Valeriya Anufriyeva/Shutterstock, 8 (background), 23br; chaoss/Shutterstock, 8 (strawberries), 23br; KK Tan/Shutterstock, 9; baburkina/Deposit Photos, 10–11; India Picture/Shutterstock, 12–13; Sergey Novikov/Shutterstock, 14–15; Sean Prior/Alamy, 17; KPG_Payless/Shutterstock, 18–19; New Africa/Shutterstock, 22; Image Source/iStock, 23tl; Veronica Louro/Shutterstock, 24.

Printed in the United States of America at Corporate Graphics in North Mankato, Minnesota.

Table of Contents

Friends Are Fair	4
Practice Being Fair	22
Picture Glossary	23
Index	24
To Learn More	24

Friends Are Fair

We are fair.
How?

We treat everyone the same.
We share.

Hope and Jude have four stickers.

Each gets two.

This is fair.

**Tia has five strawberries.
Jen only has three.**

Tia shares one with Jen.
Now they both have four.
This is fair.

Tim plays with cars.
His brother wants to play, too.
Tim lets him.

Being fair means more.
Jae doesn't lie.
Even to help herself.
That would be unfair.

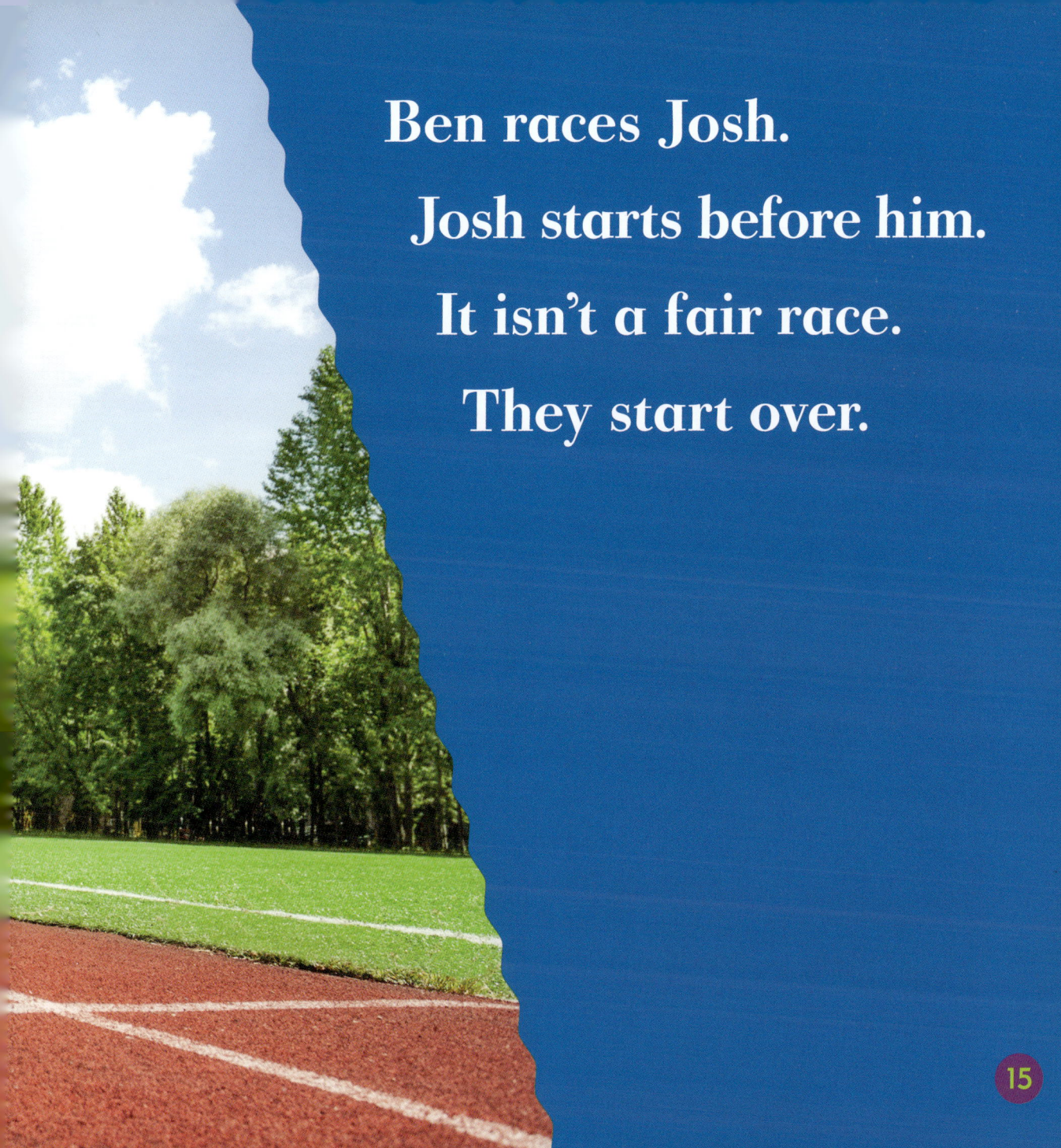

Ben races Josh.
Josh starts before him.
It isn't a fair race.
They start over.

Piñata Rules

1. Place a blindfold over your eyes. Don't peek!

2. Spin three times.

3. Try to hit and break open the piñata!

Jake and Ty play a game. They follow the rules.

We play baseball.

Everyone has a turn to bat.

Nice!

We share.

We treat others how we want to be treated.

We are fair.

Practice Being Fair

Sometimes being fair is hard. It helps to practice!

Gather 10 of the same items. Practice dividing them up fairly. How would you divide them if there were two people? How would you divide them if there were five people? What would you do if you couldn't divide them evenly?

Picture Glossary

cheat
To get something in a dishonest way.

fair
Something that is equal or just.

share
To divide something equally between two or more people.

unfair
Something that is not fair or equal.

Index

cheat 17
fair 4, 6, 9, 12, 15, 21
lie 12
plays 11, 16, 18
races 15
rules 16

same 5
share 5, 9, 21
stickers 6
strawberries 8
turn 18
unfair 12

To Learn More

Finding more information is as easy as 1, 2, 3.

❶ Go to www.factsurfer.com

❷ Enter "beingfair" into the search box.

❸ Click the "Surf" button to see a list of websites.